The Sun
and the Seasons

by Peggy Bresnick Kendler

PEARSON
Scott
Foresman

What You Already Know

Day, night, and seasons are caused by the movements of Earth and light from the Sun. The Sun is a star.

Earth rotates around an imaginary line called its axis. Earth makes one whole rotation every twenty-four hours. It appears as if the Sun moves across the sky during the day. But it is really Earth that moves.

While Earth rotates, it also moves around the Sun. Each trip around the Sun is called

a revolution. A complete revolution takes about 365 days, or one year. Seasons are caused by Earth's tilt and movement around the Sun.

Earth revolves around the Sun.

While Earth moves around the Sun, the Moon moves around Earth. The Moon has a slightly different appearance, or phase, each night. An eclipse of the Moon, or lunar eclipse, happens when the Moon moves behind the Earth,

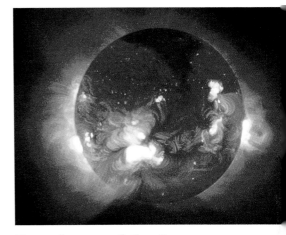

X-ray image of the Sun

which blocks sunlight from reaching the Moon.

At night there are stars in the sky. A telescope is used to see stars more clearly. The constellations are patterns made by stars.

Earth and the Sun work together in many interesting ways. They interact to create day and night, the seasons, and shadows. Read on to find out all about the Sun and how it affects Earth!

Earth in Space

Earth and the Sun work together to create seasons and give us day and night. Without the Sun, Earth would be dark and cold. We have seasons because the Earth tilts as it moves around the Sun. We have days and nights because of the way Earth rotates on its axis as it makes its way around the Sun.

We cannot feel Earth's movements. Still, our planet is always rotating and moving around the Sun. The path Earth follows around the Sun is called its orbit. Earth is part of the solar system. The solar system is made up of eight planets. Each of the planets is different from Earth in many ways. However, all the solar system's planets revolve around the Sun.

Earth is one of eight planets in our solar system that revolves around the Sun.

Earth is the third-closest planet to the Sun. It is the fourth largest of all the planets. Mercury is the hottest planet and the closest to the Sun. Venus is between Earth and Mercury. The other five planets are farther away from the Sun and are much colder than Earth.

The Solar System

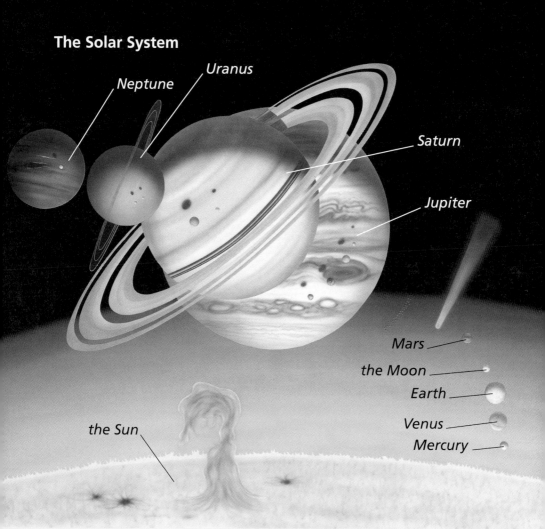

Neptune

Uranus

Saturn

Jupiter

Mars

the Moon

Earth

Venus

Mercury

the Sun

The Sun

The Sun is a star. Compared to other stars, it has an average size, brightness, and mass. It is the closest star to Earth. That makes it appear much larger and brighter than other stars.

The Sun is about 150 million kilometers from Earth. It is much, much bigger than Earth. You would have to place 109 Earths side by side to equal the Sun's diameter!

The Sun is the source of practically all Earth's energy. Nothing could live on our planet without its rays.

The Sun's huge size gives it a strong gravitational pull. This keeps the planets in our solar system orbiting around the Sun.

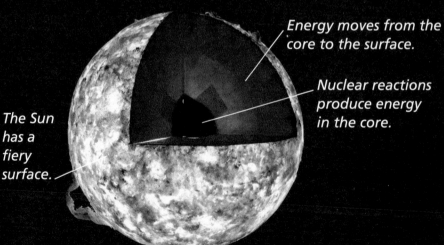

Energy moves from the core to the surface.

Nuclear reactions produce energy in the core.

The Sun has a fiery surface.

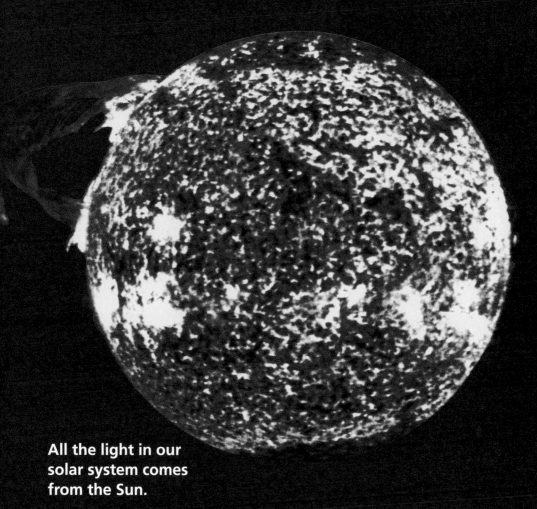

All the light in our solar system comes from the Sun.

The Sun is at least four and a half billion years old. It is a huge, rotating ball of hot gas. Energy is released within the Sun's central core. The core, at twenty-seven million degrees Fahrenheit, is the hottest part of the Sun. Energy moves from the Sun's core to its surface. From there it travels into space. This energy provides light and heat for the surfaces of Earth and the solar system's other planets.

Earth's Orbit

Our solar system's planets orbit the Sun. Gravity keeps Earth moving in its path around the Sun. Earth travels around the Sun in an oval-shaped path called an ellipse. This ellipse places Earth closer to the Sun in January than in July.

Earth's elliptical orbit, which was first described by the astronomer Johannes Kepler, changes shape over time. These changes make the sunlight on Earth either stronger or weaker, and may affect Earth's climate.

Earth orbits the Sun in an oval-shaped path called an ellipse.

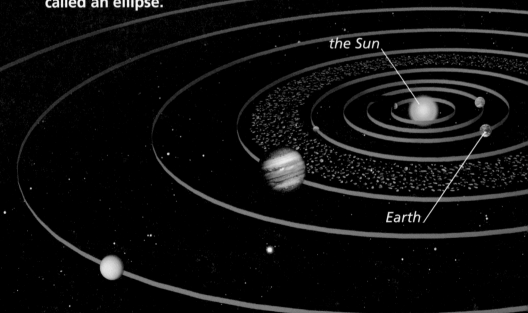

the Sun

Earth

Planets that are closer to the Sun have shorter orbits. They take less time to orbit the Sun. Because of that, years are much shorter on these planets.

Mercury is the closest planet to the Sun. Its year is only about 87 days. Neptune is farthest from the Sun. Its year is 60,223 days long! The closest planet to Earth is Venus. Venus has a year that lasts about 225 days. That equals approximately three-fifths of an Earth year.

Charting the Sun

The Medicine Wheel is a circular rock formation in Wyoming. It is believed that long ago Native Americans used it as a calendar.

The Seasons

In your mind, draw a line from the North Pole to the South Pole. Have it run through Earth's core. Scientists call this imaginary line Earth's axis. Earth tilts on its axis, making one side slant toward the Sun. This slant is what causes seasons.

The equator is an imaginary line that circles Earth. It is midway between the North Pole and the South Pole. The equator divides Earth into two equal parts, or hemispheres. It is always sunny and warm along the equator.

the seasons

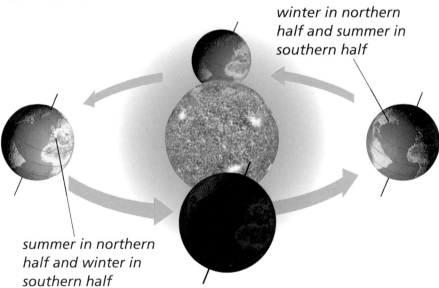

winter in northern half and summer in southern half

summer in northern half and winter in southern half

When it's winter in New York, it's summer in Australia.

In December, Earth's Northern Hemisphere slants away from the Sun. This causes winter in the United States. At the same time, summertime happens in the Southern Hemisphere. That's because the Southern Hemisphere is slanted toward the Sun in December.

In June, Earth's Northern Hemisphere tilts toward the Sun. This causes summertime in the United States. At the same time, Earth's Southern Hemisphere tilts away from the Sun. This causes winter in countries in the Southern Hemisphere, such as Australia.

Earth is tilted at an angle of 23.5 degrees. This angle, like Earth's orbit, changes over time. Changes to Earth's tilt can affect its climate.

Solstices and Equinoxes

The days of the year with the greatest difference betwen day and night are the solstices. The days of the year with nearly equal amounts of daylight and darkness are the equinoxes.

There are two solstices each year. The summer solstice is around June 21 in the Northern Hemisphere. The Northern Hemisphere gets the most sunlight this day. The winter solstice is around December 21 in the Northern Hemisphere. The Northern Hemisphere gets the least amount of sunlight this day.

Stonehenge is an ancient stone monument in England. People long ago may have used it as a clock, calendar, or for ceremonies.

Equinoxes happen twice each year, just like solstices. During the equinoxes, the rays of sunlight fall directly on the equator. This means the Northern and Southern Hemispheres have the same amount of daylight and darkness. Both hemispheres have twelve hours of daylight and darkness.

Midnight Sun

Bodo is a place in northern Norway. The Sun doesn't disappear for an entire month there during summer.

Eclipses

A solar eclipse happens when the Moon passes directly between Earth and the Sun. The Moon's shadow blocks sunlight from reaching Earth. After a few minutes Earth passes out of the Moon's shadow. Then the Sun reappears.

A lunar eclipse happens when the Moon passes behind Earth. Earth blocks sunlight from reaching the Moon. Earth's shadow covers the Moon. After a few minutes the Moon passes out of Earth's shadow. Then the Moon becomes visible again from Earth.

You should never look directly at the Sun. The Sun's rays are powerful enough to damage your eyes.

It is especially dangerous to look at the Sun during a solar eclipse. You might think it is safe to look at a solar eclipse because the Moon blocks the Sun's rays. But the rays that remain unblocked are still too bright! You need to wear special sunglasses to watch a solar eclipse.

Special sunglasses make it safe for people to view an eclipse.

Day and Night

Half of Earth is always facing the Sun. So half of Earth always has daylight. At the same time, half of Earth always faces away from the Sun. So half of Earth always has darkness.

Every twenty-four hours, Earth completes a full rotation on its axis. Because of that, all of Earth gets a full 24 hour day, every day.

Part of Earth always faces the Sun, while the rest of the planet is in darkness.

When it is daytime in Sydney, Australia, it is nighttime in the United States.

Earth turns very fast on its axis. Different parts of Earth rotate at different rates of speed. At the equator, the speed of rotation is 470 meters per second!

As night falls in New York, the Sun appears on the other side of Earth.

However, Earth rotates very slowly at the poles. A person standing at either of the poles goes "nowhere." But think about a person standing at the equator. The day is twenty-four hours long. Multiply that by the speed of Earth's rotation at the equator, which is 1,050 miles per hour. People living on the equator "go" 25,000 miles in a day! Despite this, people living on the equator can't feel Earth rotating. In fact, no one on Earth can!

The Rotating Earth

Earth's axis points in the same direction as the planet revolves around the Sun. The axis points toward the North Star. The North Star is also called Polaris. "Polaris" refers to its location in the night sky above the North Pole. To people on Earth, Polaris remains in the same place in the sky year after year. Polaris has helped people travel in the Northern Hemisphere for thousands of years.

Polaris cannot be seen in the Southern Hemisphere at night. The Earth blocks the Southern Hemisphere from seeing it. Unlike the Northern Hemisphere, the Southern Hemisphere does not have a star that appears to stay in place.

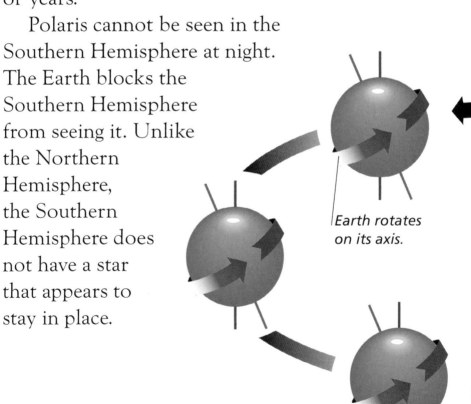

Earth rotates on its axis.

Earth continually moves in two different ways. It rotates on its axis and revolves around the Sun. If Earth stopped rotating, there would be 6 months of daylight, followed by 6 months of night. If Earth stopped revolving, there would be no changing seasons.

Earth in Motion

Earth is in constant motion, even though we are not aware of it. We don't feel Earth moving because everything else is moving at the same time.

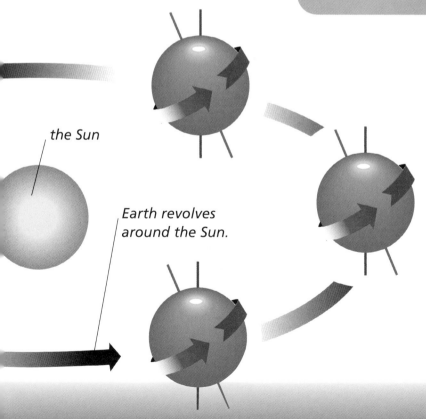

the Sun

Earth revolves around the Sun.

Shadows

Earth spins on its axis in a counterclockwise direction. Because of the way it spins, the Sun always appears in the east and disappears in the west.

At noon the Sun is at its highest point in the sky. The shadows at noon are very short. They do not reach very far.

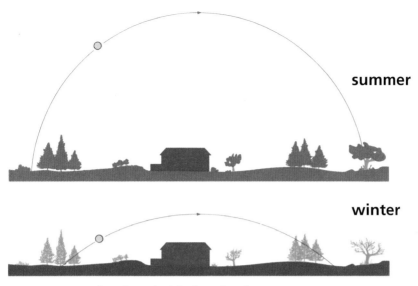

summer

winter

In summer, the Sun is higher in the sky than in winter.

The shadows made by the Sun are longest at sunrise and sunset. In the morning, shadows point to the west. This is because the Sun appears in the east. During the afternoon, shadows stretch to the east. This is because the Sun disappears into the west.

The lengths of shadows change, depending on the time of year and where the Sun is in the sky. Shadows are longest during a midwinter's day. That's when the Sun is lowest in the sky. Shadows are shortest at noon during the summer. That's when the Sun is directly overhead.

A sundial tells time using shadows made by sunlight.

The Sun and Earth

The Sun is at the center of our solar system. The Sun and Earth work together to bring our planet days and nights. They also work together to give us different seasons. Earth is always moving, both on its axis and around the Sun.

The Sun is just one star among many in the universe. But it is the star that we depend on! The energy that comes from its gases supports life. That energy allows plants to grow. It keeps people and Earth's other living things warm.

The next time you walk outside on a sunny day, you might think of the Sun in a new way. Think about the Sun's important role in our daily lives. Where would life be without it?

Earth's rotation causes the Sun to disappear beneath the sky at sunset.

Glossary

ellipse   a shape that looks like a stretched circle

equator   an imaginary line circling Earth between the North Pole and the South Pole

equinox   the first day of spring and fall when both hemispheres have the same amount of daylight and darkness

gravitational pull   the effect of gravity on another object

hemisphere   half of a sphere, or half of Earth

orbit   the path of an object in space

solstice   the first day of winter and summer; also the shortest and longest day of the year in the Northern Hemisphere